Wine

A cultural history from around the world

Ed S. Milton

Astrolog Publishing House Ltd.

Edited by: S. Milton
Cover Design: Na'ama Yaffe
Layout and Graphics: Daniel Akerman

P.O. Box 1123, Hod Hasharon 45111, Israel
Tel: 972-9-7412044
Fax: 972-9-7442714

© Astrolog Publishing House Ltd. 2003

ISBN 965-494-161-9

All rights reserved. No part of this publication may be reproduced, stored in a retrieval system, or transmitted, in any form or by any means, electronic, mechanical, photocopying, recording or otherwise, without the prior permission of the publisher.

Published by Astrolog Publishing House 2003

10 9 8 7 6 5 4 3 2 1

Wine

The wild vine from which man cultivated the grapevine was one of the first agricultural crops. The wild vine appeared nearly three million years ago. Some 25,000 years ago, man already knew about gathering the bunches of grapes from the wild vines and extracting their juice. (Seeds from grapes that had been crushed with heavy stones have been found in archeological excavations.) Some 15,000 years ago, farmers began to raise and cultivate the wild vine. This vine, the olive tree and the fig tree were the first plants to be cultivated by man during the transition from ambulant hunter to sedentary farmer.

Wine

The grapevine (Vitis vinifera) appeared in Kafkaz in the eighth century BC. Two thousand years later, we find stone pestles, special earthenware jars for storing wine, and even decorations consisting of bunches of grapes on the jars.

Wine

*I*n the Tigris and Euphrates region, about 5,000 years ago, inscriptions describing wine production were found, as were tablets that described drinking wine from goblets. The wine was kept in leather bags. During the same period, we find earthenware jars containing wine in Egypt placed in graves containing mummies, and paintings and reliefs depicting the raising and harvesting of the bunches of grapes as well as the process of juice extraction.

Wine

Four thousand years ago, earthenware jars containing wine began to appear in Egypt. On them, there were seals attesting to the year of harvest and place of the harvest as well as the producer of the wine. Those were actually the first wine labels.

Wine

*I*n Babylon, 4,000 years ago, the fate of anyone who diluted wine with water or who cheated on the amount of wine in the jar he sold, was death. The sentence was carried out by the king's executioners, who would sew the unfortunate vintner into a donkey skin along with heavy stones and cast him into the river.

Wine

Wine appears frequently in the Bible and the New Testament. Occasionally, it appears in the context of lechery and drunkenness – Noah emerging from the Ark, getting drunk and displaying his nakedness, or Lot becoming inebriated and having sex with his daughters. On the other hand, wine appears in the context of sacred wine that is offered as an offering to the Temple. In both cases – wine as a source of lechery or as a holy offering – an abundance of wine and grapevines is described as a sign of a thriving economy.

Wine

And Noah began to be an husbandman, and he planted a vineyard: And he drank of the wine, and was drunken; and he was uncovered within his tent. And Ham, the father of Canaan, saw the nakedness of his father, and told his two brethren without. And Shem and Ja'pheth took a garment, and laid it upon both their shoulders, and went backward, and covered the nakedness of their father; and their faces were backward, and they saw not their father's nakedness. And Noah awoke from his wine, and knew what his younger son had done unto him.

GENESIS, Chap. 9, 20-24

Wine

Come, let us make our father drink wine, and we will lie with him, that we may preserve seed of our father. And they made their father drink wine that night: and the firstborn went in, and lay with her father; and he perceived not when she lay down, nor when she arose. And it came to pass on the morrow, that the firstborn said unto the younger, Behold, I lay yesternight with my father; let us make him drink wine this night also; and go thou in, and lie with him, that we may preserve seed of our father. And they made their father drink wine that night also; and the younger arose, and lay with him; and he perceived nor when she lay down, nor when she arose. Thus were both the daughters of Lot with child by their father.

GENESIS, Chap. 19, 32-36

Wine

And the chief butler told his dream to Joseph, and said to him, in my dream, behold, a vine was before me; And in the vine there were three branches: and it was as though it budded, and her blossoms shot forth; and the clusters thereof brought forth ripe grapes: And Pharaoh's cup was in my hand: and I took the grapes, and pressed them into Pharaoh's cup, and I gave the cup into Pharaoh's hand. And Joseph said unto him, This is the interpretation of it: The three branches are three days: Yet within three days shall Pharaoh lift up thine head, and restore thee unto thy place: and thou shalt deliver Pharaoh's cup into his hand, after the former manner when thou wast his butler.

GENESIS, Chap. 40, 9-13

Wine

*I*n every mythological story in every culture, wine is the link between the gods and human beings. In many myths, the gods – Osiris in Egypt, Dionysos in Greece, and so on – bring wine to human beings, and generally drink with them. In many cases, the drinking turns into an orgy of lechery.

Wine

*I*n ancient Babylon, the wine merchant was part of sacred prostitution (women who served as temple prostitutes prior to their marriage) system. The clients would purchase a goblet of wine and get a woman for dessert. This happy arrangement stemmed from the religious belief that a sacred prostitute was not supposed to receive remuneration for her services in the temple.

Wine

A Persian legend calls wine "the water from the feet of the princess," and the story goes like this: A princess who was brought to the king's palace pined for the love of her youth who had remained behind in the castle. In order to reach him, she slipped into a gigantic jar in which bunches of grapes were transported from the king's palace to his storerooms. While she was in the jar, she crushed the grapes with her feet, and, being thirsty, she drank the juice. The juice from the grapes cheered her up and she burst into song…

Wine

and that's how the palace guards discovered her. When they brought the princess to the king, she gave him a goblet containing "the water from her feet" from the huge jar. The king, curious and amazed to see the princess who was not afraid of losing her head, drank from the goblet… and from that day on, wine, "the water from the feet of the princess," became the drink of kings.

Wine

In ancient Greece, according to Homer, wine was mixed with water. The superb wine was red wine, powerful and intoxicating, and it came from Thrace. The most famous property of red wine, according to Homer, was… the headache from which the person suffered after a night of drinking. In contrast, wine that originated from Chianos was light red wine, which boasted the property of "not causing a headache after drinking it."

Wine

Wine from Cos is white, and the ancient Greeks would mix it with… seawater. This wine was dedicated to the god of the sea, Poseidon.

Wine

The wine industry in ancient Greece commenced some 4,000 years ago and reached its peak in the fifth century BC. Gods and human beings raised vineyards, harvested grapes and produced wines. Paintings, reliefs and mosaics depict orgies and festivities featuring wine-drinking as their focal point. Anakrion wrote his famous wine songs and Hesiudos wrote poetry describing the vintner's work and the production of wine.

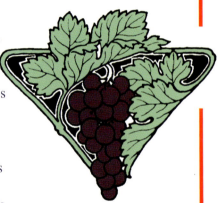

Wine

*O*enotria, the land of wine, was the name given to southern Italy. At the time of the birth of Jesus of Nazareth, vineyards and winemaking were so profitable in Italy that a severe shortage of wheat, olives and vegetables developed. Roman soldiers, who received plots of land in conquered territories (such as in France), also hastened to plant vines... and Rome was forced to conquer Egypt in order to import wheat and vegetables from there.

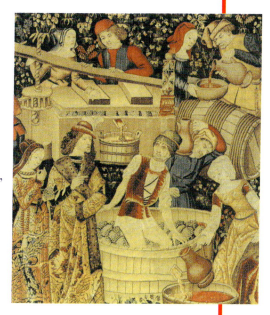

Wine

The Roman leaders required prodigious amounts of wine as a result of the order that the Roman soldier's wages included a skin of wine for every week of service. A skin of wine contained 11 liters of wine, generally sour wine (Posca) that was not intoxicating. The soldiers were prepared to postpone receiving the monetary payment for their service, but the Roman general who did not supply the necessary amounts of wine needed a fast horse to escape from the wrath of his soldiers.

Wine

The life of Jesus and the whole of the New Testament are interwoven with wine. Jesus turned water into wine, and at the Last Supper, he sipped from the cup of wine and let all the Apostles drink from it, saying: "This is my blood." After his death, wine became a central component in the Christian ritual.

Wine

The centrality of wine in the Christian ritual led Christians and churches to cultivate vines and produce wine. In the fifth century, in which the vineyards of Europe collapsed following the Barbarian invasions and the subsequent torching of the vineyards, the hegemony over wine shifted to the Christian monasteries. Only in the ninth century AD did the rulers of Europe begin to encourage the planting of vineyards and the production of wine, and the monopoly passed from the church to the rulers and big merchants.

Wine

China, Japan and other Eastern countries prefer wine based on… rice! The reason for this is a practical one: vineyards require large expanses of land, and in countries where the population is large and crowded and tracts of lands are in short supply, it is preferable to grow rice or grains such as wheat and soya.

Wine

*I*n the 15th century, heavy taxes were imposed on wine merchants who imported wines from Greece or from Asia Minor to England. The number of inns where wine was served was limited, and the man in the street (the non-nobleman, in other words) could only keep a "bucketful" (about four liters) of wine in his cellar.

Wine

Columbus and his comrades brought wine to the New World, but the wild vine had been known in North America long before Columbus' time. Vineland, the vine coast, was the name given to the Massachusetts coast by the Vikings. The first settlers to begin producing wine in America were the Huguenots – Frenchmen who settled in Florida. Initially, they used wild vines, but later they had strains from Europe brought over and grafted them onto the wild vines that grew in America. In the 17th century, Franciscan monks began to establish vineyards in California.

By the end of the 19th century, vine cuttings were imported to America from Europe. In appreciation of the import of the vine cuttings, America exported to Europe a parasite called the *Phylloxera* louse that lives on the American wild vine. This louse did not harm the wild vine, but it annihilated almost all the European vineyards in the mid-19th century. In France, 98% of the vineyards were destroyed within five years. America, which had inflicted the plague, also supplied the remedy – American wild vines upon which grapevines had been grafted. Ships loaded with American wild vine cuttings were sent to Europe in order to rehabilitate the wine industry there.

Wine

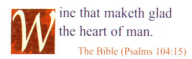

Wine that maketh glad the heart of man.

The Bible (Psalms 104:15)

Wine

There is no agriculture process in which the importance of the "worker" is greater than in the case of wine production. The vintner, who supervises the production of the wine, is involved in the process from the selection of the plot of land, the planting of the cuttings, the cultivation of the vines and the harvesting of the grapes to the extraction of the juice, the fermentation process and the aging of the wine.

 Wine

Famous vintners earn the privilege of having the product, the wine, named after them. It is also interesting to discover that the basic process of cultivating the vines and making the wine has remained identical for thousands of years – in fact, the manuals that were written in ancient Rome or medieval France are studied in schools for vintners to this day.

Wine

The production process is very simple: bunches of grapes are harvested, transported to a wine cellar for the extraction of their juice, and are fermented in containers or pools. During the fermentation process, the sugar contained in the grape turns into alcohol as a result of the presence of natural yeasts on the grapes. The control and regulation of the fermentation process is in fact what determines the eventual type and quality of the wine.

After the fermentation stage, the wine is strained, and then is either poured into barrels for aging or poured into bottles. A simple process, but, as a famous French vintner said, "With the help of several dozen letters and signs, we can get the best (French) poetry and literature… or a horrendous and meaningless jumble of words. The vintner is the poet, the author, the one who turns the meaningless letters into a work of art."

Wine

Every type of wine is, in fact, grape juice that has undergone a certain process. We find white, red or rosé wines; we find dry, sweet or "semi-sweet" wines; we find wines with a 5% alcohol content – and wines with a 20% alcohol content. They all have the same source in common: grapes!

*I*n various places in the world, we find "wines" produced from different crops, such as rice wine or date wine. With all due respect to those wines, this book only deals with wine that comes from grapes.

Wine

Amateur vintners grow vines by themselves or purchase bunches of grapes from vineyards or markets. Since there are several thousand strains of wine grapes, knowing them and their properties is a complicated matter. However, it is possible to learn a few basic rules:

- *If the grapes are large and juicy, their essence and flavor are pale.*
- *The smaller the grapes, the more concentrated their flavor.*
- *The skin of the grape determines the color of the wine.*
- *In addition to color, the skin is the source of the tannin in the wine.*
- *The sweeter the grape, the higher the level of alcohol will be.*

Wine

A fungus by the name of *Botrytis cinevea*, which is also called "Noble Rot," develops on bunches of grapes on hot days (over 20°C/68°F) and causes the grapes to pucker. In this situation, the grapes are strong and sweet, and the wine produced from them is sweeter.

 Wine

*C*ome, eat of my bread, and drink of the wine which I have mingled.

PROVERBS, Chap. 9, 5

Ice wine, which comes from Germany (*Eisewein*) and France (*vin de gêlée*), is wine that is made from frozen bunches of grapes. The first ice wines resulted from a sudden freeze, which compelled the vintners to harvest frozen grapes. Today, there are vineyards (in Canada, for instance) where the vintners delay the harvest until the temperature drops and the grapes freeze. Experiments have also been conducted to freeze grapes (for 48 hours) and then to extract their juice. In these cases, too, the resulting wine is especially sweet and fragrant.

Wine

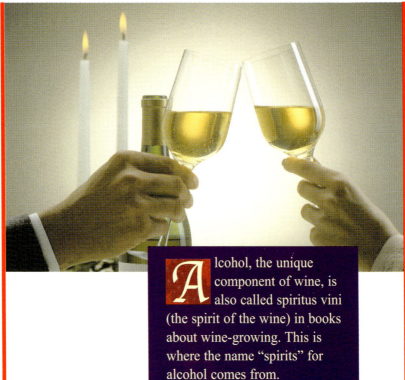

Alcohol, the unique component of wine, is also called spiritus vini (the spirit of the wine) in books about wine-growing. This is where the name "spirits" for alcohol comes from.

Wine

In ancient Rome, it was forbidden for women to drink wine. It was believed that a woman who drank a goblet of wine would lose her sense of modesty and would be prepared to commit every possible act of adultery (perhaps that's the reason why men tried to ply women with wine). In the second century AD, laws were proposed in the Roman Senate, stating that "a man who finds his wife drinking wine and cuts her head off will not be considered a murderer." In another case, "a woman who drinks wine in public will have her lips sewn up and she will be buried alive." Both proposals were rejected, incidentally.

Wine

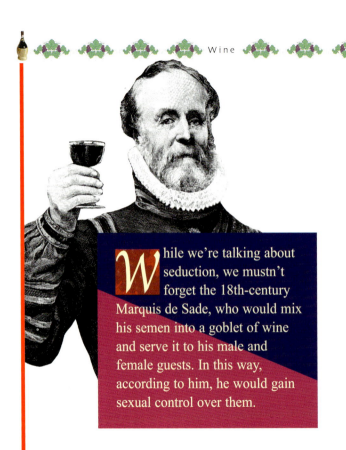

While we're talking about seduction, we mustn't forget the 18th-century Marquis de Sade, who would mix his semen into a goblet of wine and serve it to his male and female guests. In this way, according to him, he would gain sexual control over them.

Wine

The honorable Pope Paul III (he was pope for 15 years in the 16th century) was a very virile fornicator who was in the habit of washing his private parts in sweet red wine every evening. He did this more and more and would sell the wine – after washing in it – as wine with unique healing properties. The belief that washing one's penis in wine reinforces virility is quite widespread. The Frenchman, Apollinaire, relates in his memoirs that while he was a student at the university, he and his friends would rinse their penises in red wine before sallying forth to the "red light" districts of Paris.

Wine

case (*caisse*) of wine is a custom that is maintained between wine merchants. A case contains 12 standard bottles of wine – 750 ml each.

Wine

*I*n many churches in Europe, it is customary to say prayers that are known by the name of "wine songs." The aim of these prayers, which are accompanied by the ringing of the church bells, is to prevent hail – since heavy hail is the greatest enemy of the vineyards of Europe! The vine and the grapes cannot withstand the hail, and heavy hail can destroy not only the crop of an entire year, but it can damage the crops of the coming years. In addition to the prayers and the bells, it was customary in Europe to shoot cannonballs into the air above the vineyards, or light tall bonfires.

Wine

In ancient Egypt, Persia, Greece and ancient Rome, it was customary to wash the warriors' wounds on the battlefield in wine, in the belief that washing in wine would heal the wounds and help them knit.

Wine

*I*n ancient Egypt and Greece, when people wanted to drink murky water, it was customary to mix the water with… wine! This custom was widespread mainly on board ship, where the water that was stored in jars or in leather skins was undrinkable.

Wine

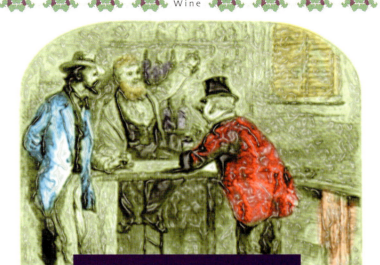

Grog is heated wine to which raisins, almonds and brandy (burned wine) are added. The beverage is widespread mainly in the cold northern European countries and in North America.

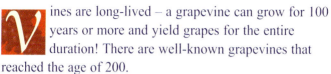 Wine

Vines are long-lived – a grapevine can grow for 100 years or more and yield grapes for the entire duration! There are well-known grapevines that reached the age of 200.

Hear another parable: There was a certain householder, which planted a vineyard, and hedged it round about, and digged a winepress in it, and built a tower, and let it out to husbandmen, and went into a far country: And when the time of the fruit drew near, he sent his servants to the husbandmen, that they might receive the fruits of it. And the husbandmen took his servants, and beat one, and killed another, and stones another. Again, he sent other servants more than the first: and they did unto them likewise. But last of all he sent unto them his son, saying, They will reverence my son. But when the husbandmen saw the son, they said among themselves, This is the heir; come, let us kill him, and let us seize on his inheritance. And they caught him, and cast him out of the vineyard, and slew him. When the lord therefore of the vineyard cometh, what will he do unto those husbandmen? They say unto him, He will miserably destroy those wicked men, and will let out his vineyard unto other husbandmen, which shall render him the fruits in their seasons.

MATTHEW, Chap. 21, 33-41

Wine

Neither do men put new wine into old bottles: else the bottles break, and the wine runneth out, and the bottles perish: but they put new wine into new bottles, and both are preserved.

MATTHEW, Chap. 9, 17

Wine

 nd went to him, and bound up his wounds, pouring in oil and wine, and set him on his own beast, and brought him to an inn, and took care of him.

LUKE, Chap. 10, 34

Wine

They that tarry long at the wine; they that go to seek mixed wine. Look not thou upon the wine when it is red, when it giveth his color in the cup, when it moveth itself aright.

PROVERBS, Chap. 23, 30-31

Wine

*T*herefore hear now this, thou afflicted, and drunken, but not with wine.

ISAIAH, Chap. 51, 21

Wine

 ine gives great pleasure, and every pleasure is of itself a good.

Samuel Johnson

Wine

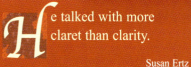

He talked with more claret than clarity.

Susan Ertz

Wine

Claret is the liquor for boys; port for men; but he who aspires to be a hero must drink brandy.

Samuel Johnson

Wine

ne of the disadvantages of wine is that it makes a man mistake words for thoughts.

Samuel Johnson

Wine

iogenes was asked what wine he liked best; and he answered as I would have done when he said: "Somebody else's"

Michel de Montaigne

Wine

The wine of Arpad Haraszthy has a bouquet all its own. It tickles and titillates the palate. It gurgles as it slips down the alimentary canal. It warms the cockles of the heart, and it burns the sensitive lining of the stomach.

Ambrose Bierce

Wine

o poems can live long or please that are written by water-drinkers.

Horace

Wine

t's a naive wine without breeding, but I think you'll be amused by its presumption.

James Thurber

 Wine

 hoped to drown my sorrows in wine, but the wine just makes them heavier.

Li Tai Fu, 701-762

Wine

Do you ask for your life to move on a good path? Do you want to get away from sorrow? Then never give up, not for a moment, on a drink of wine.

Omar Khayyim

To see far into the distance, better wine than the eye.

Calman Meroux

Wine

"You will not find a nobleman who hates a good wine."

Francois Rable

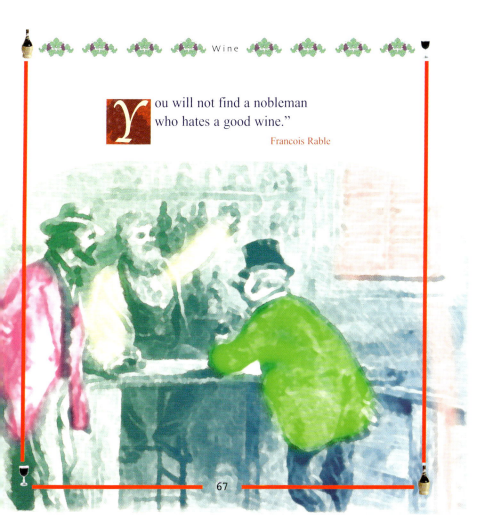

Wine

> "God created water – but man made wine."
>
> Victor Hugo

Wine

 know of only two things that improve with age – wine and lovers.

Lupe de Vega

Wine

He who does not know how to drink, does not know how to love; but the drinkers among you must know that he who does not know how to love, does not know how to drink.

Johan Wolfgang von Geta

Wine

 n one bottle of wine, there is more philosophy than in all of the books combined.

Louis Pasteur

Wine

Wine is the intellectual part of a banquet.

Alexandre Dumas

Wine

The vine alone, of all of the plant life, bestows the clear taste of the earth. Through its grapes, the vine is the earth's loyal translator of its secrets.

Colette

 Wine

ine is the son of the sun and the earth, it releases the spirit and awakens the sensibilities.

Paul Claudel

 Wine

 he soul of each house is found in its winecellar.

Ramon Gomez de la Serana

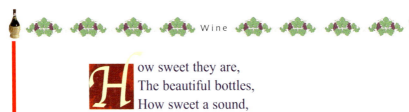

Wine

How sweet they are,
The beautiful bottles,
How sweet a sound,
Glug-glug-glug.
My fate would be the envy of all,
If full you'd always be,
On holy days and days of the week.
Why do you ever get empty?

Moliere

Wine

A Greek myth relates that Dionysos, the god of wine, was the one who gave man the grapevine. One day, Dionysos found a piece of a young branch and he hid it in a bird's bone. He hid the bird's bone in a lion's bone, the lion's bone in a donkey's bone… and he buried the donkey's bone in the earth. The first grapevine grew in that place. Therefore, when a person drinks one glass of wine, his head is lighter than a bird's. When he drinks two glasses of wine, he is filled with a lion's courage, and when he drinks three glasses of wine, he behaves lasciviously like a donkey (the donkey is the symbol of sexual depravity in ancient Greece).

Wine

The saying, "Every soldier carries the general's baton in his kitbag," is well known. What is less well known is the fact that the origin of this saying is in the Roman witticism from the days of Julius Caesar, which says the "Every soldier carries a vine branch in his kitbag…," a witticism that was prevalent during the period when the Romans planted vineyards in all the places they conquered.

Wine

Troy fell to the Greeks thanks to the Trojan Horse trick … but we must not forget that, according to various sources, the Greeks brought numerous jars of wine as well as the horse, causing the Trojans to get drunk.

Wine

*S*piced wine is what caused the Cyclops, who was holding Odysseus and his companions in a cave, to fall into a deep sleep, enabling Odysseus to blind his single eye and then escape from the cave.

During the period of Prohibition in the United States (1919-1932), there was an increase of 20 times in the output of vineyards that received permission to produce wine for purposes of religious rituals.

 Wine

*I*n Egypt, the art of building pergolas developed. The vines climbed over the pergolas and created an awning that protected the bunches of grapes and prevented the ground from drying up. The art of building pergolas spread from Egypt to other Middle Eastern countries. In other places, the art of training the vines developed in parallel. This involved the use of posts and ropes in order to direct the growth of the weave of the vine.

Wine

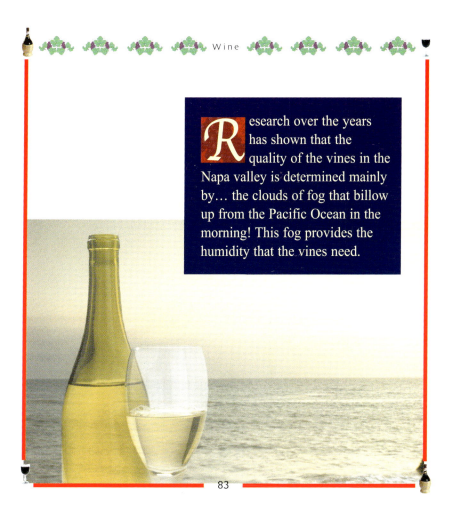

Research over the years has shown that the quality of the vines in the Napa valley is determined mainly by... the clouds of fog that billow up from the Pacific Ocean in the morning! This fog provides the humidity that the vines need.

Wine

*E*very European vintner gets up in the morning, and before he drinks a cup of coffee, he checks – in the newspaper or on the radio or the TV – the conditions of the terroir, the conditions for growing vines and producing wine. These conditions include temperature, humidity, wind and clouds as well as ground and location conditions.

Wine

he Australian continent is becoming the new bonanza for aficionados of wine. The first vineyards in Australia were planted at the end of the 18th century. The big advantage of vineyards in Australia lies in the stable weather conditions that ensure that the crops are uniform over the years. The annual per capita wine consumption in Australia is not particularly high, and most of the production is for export. Experts claim that in ten years' time, Australia, together with South Africa and Chile, will vie for top place in wine production in the world.

Wine

The largest wine producer in the world is still Italy. It has seven times more vineyard area than Australia (and its annual per capita wine consumption is three times higher than in Australia). In Italy, we find most types of wine, and the simple guiding rule for buyers is: the further north the vineyard or the cellar, the better the wine… and much more expensive.

Wine

The later the bunches of grapes are harvested, the smaller the amount of water in the grapes and the greater the percentage of sugar. Early harvesting results in a low sugar content.

Wine

Grapes are traditionally harvested manually, usually by workers who specialize in this art. This means that the bunches are examined and harvested one at a time, and reach the wine cellars clean and unblemished. Nowadays, mechanical harvesters are used, and while they are effective and inexpensive, the quality of the grapes that reach the wine cellars is poor in comparison to those that are harvested manually.

The color of the grape skin determines the color of the wine – white or red. Having said that, it is possible to produce white wine from "red" grapes if their skins are removed. This is done in the production of champagne, for instance, which traditionally contains about 50% "red" grapes.

Wine

Sherry is actually wine that has a much higher alcohol content than regular wines, but it belongs to the department of spirits.

Wine

(Good) sweet wines are sometimes up to 50% more expensive than "dry" or "semi sweet" wines. This is mainly because the production of (good) sweet wine requires an especially lengthy and demanding production process.

Wine

The imbibing of sweet wine is usually accompanied by the consumption of cheese – especially hard cheese. We find that an increase in the consumption of sweet wine is accompanied by a commensurate increase in the consumption of hard cheeses. Also, in regions where there are excellent wine cellars, there are always dairies that produce excellent hard cheese as well.

Wine

Excellent champagne requires stable and fixed storage conditions. You need only deviate from the fixed conditions for three hours to spoil the champagne and lower its value. So, if you acquire your own wine cellar, begin the experiment with wines and move on to champagne only after you have acquired knowledge.

Wine

*I*t is well known that wine "breathes" through the cork. What is less well known is that this "breathing" can transmit odors to the wine itself. Wine must therefore not be stored in places where there are pungent odors. On the other hand, there are several wine cellars in Australia where bottles of wine are stored in a pile of eucalyptus branches. The vintners claim that the aroma of the leaves is transmitted to the wine and improves its taste.

Wine

When champagne is opened for you, listen carefully. You must hear a clear, loud "pop"! If you don't, it means that carbon dioxide has seeped into the bottle, and the champagne is flat and tasteless. Wine waiters sometimes cover the neck of the bottle in order to dull the noise of the cork when it is removed. Pay attention!

Wine

Champagne or sparkling wine is drunk in glasses that are called flutes or goblets. Only those glasses transmit the taste of the champagne to the drinker.

Wine

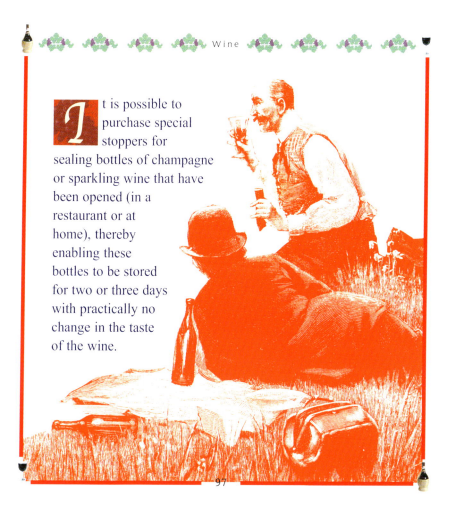

*I*t is possible to purchase special stoppers for sealing bottles of champagne or sparkling wine that have been opened (in a restaurant or at home), thereby enabling these bottles to be stored for two or three days with practically no change in the taste of the wine.

Wine

Wine experts claim that they find the highest quality bottles at bargain prices in wine warehouses or discount stores rather than in gourmet wine cellars. It transpires that wine cellars sell some of their produce to merchants in order to raise funds, and those bottles frequently reach the warehouses or discount stores.

Wine

In 2001, the most expensive red wines in the world, on average, were those from Bordeaux and Burgundy in France. The expense is mainly a result of the harvest, which is manual, and the grapes are sorted one at a time.

Wine

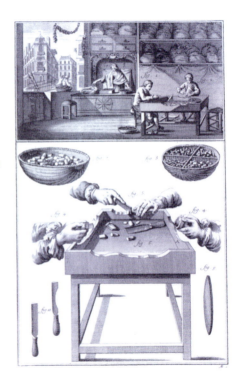

Old or flawed corks cause oxygen to seep into the wine. The wine looks "cloudy" and gourmets will never drink it.

Wine

Use your sense of smell when you are examining a bottle of wine… but first smell the cork and the open bottle. When a musty odor emanates from the bottle, or when there is a smell of vinegar, send the bottle back.

Wine

*I*n the long run, red wine keeps better than white wine. Sparkling wines have the shortest life-span.

Wine

Cooking wine must be the same quality as drinking wine! It is best to cook with the same wine as the one you are serving at the table.

Wine

As a rule of thumb, sea foods of all kinds are suitable for white wine. Gourmets prefer to serve sea foods with champagne. As for meat, the trend today is to match the color of the wine to the color of the sauce. A light sauce means white wine, while a dark sauce means red wine.

Wine

Most health experts claim that moderate wine consumption (two glasses a day for an adult) is good for the health. Many maintain that the "Mediterranean diet," which includes wine (a lot), fish, olive oil, vegetables, fruit and meat, is the healthiest diet.

A unit of alcohol" in wine means that the level of alcohol in a half-glass of wine is 8%. If there is an alcohol level of 12% in a half-glass of wine, it is "one and a half units of alcohol." (The amount of alcohol in wines ranges between 8% and 20%.)

Wine

It is recommended that men not exceed 3-4 "units of alcohol" a day, and that women not exceed 2-3 "units of alcohol" a day. (The difference in amount of alcohol between men and women stems mainly from the difference in body weight.) And watch out! In driving, even one "unit of alcohol" can endanger both driver and passengers!

Wine

The conventional belief has it that red wine is healthier than white wine. There is no scientific basis to this claim.

Wine

Hippocrates, the famous Greek physician, claimed that a mixture of equal measures of red wine and spring water could be used as a medication. In modern terms, he claimed that the medication "stimulated blood circulation."

Many experts and physicians claim that drinking half a bottle of red wine a day lowers the cholesterol levels in the blood. They base their claim on the French example – fatty food, excess weight, a lot of red wine… and relatively low cholesterol levels.

Wine

Popular belief has it that when you get up with a hangover in the morning after a night of drinking, you should drink a small glass of the last beverage you drank the previous night before passing out. There is no scientific basis to this claim.

Wine

Although wine is a beverage, it dehydrates the body. A recommendation that is always helpful is to drink a large glass of water along with every glass of wine. This prevents dehydration and hangovers, and this is the reason that a glass of water is served along with every glass of wine in restaurants.

Wine

Mixing beverages, especially wine and spirits (that is, a mixture of beverages that are based on the vine and beverages that are based on grains) is not advisable.

Wine

V*in de pays* is the French term for "wine from the region." In general, it is relatively inexpensive wine, but it is frequently "quality wine." Occasionally, this wine is called *vin de table* (table wine) in France and Europe. In other places in the world, there are similar wines, and what they all have in common is the fact that they are low-priced local wines of relatively good quality, and the main thing is that they can only be found in their area of production.

Wine

*I*n the United States, there are three regions that dominate wine production: California, Oregon and Washington. Almost 100% of the American wines are produced in these regions.

Wine

Experts stress the importance of weather conditions as well as the conditions of the climate and the soil in determining the quality of the grapes and the wine that is extracted from them. However, it must be remembered that those conditions also determine the amount of grapes, and for the vintner or the proprietor of the wine-cellar, the amount is sometimes the determining factor.

Wine

In Europe, it is claimed that the restaurateur has to sell a bottle of wine at three times the price he paid the merchant for it. In 2001, a study was conducted in which it was found that the average price is closer to five times more!

In a tasting test that was held in California between two red wines, a cheap one and a horribly expensive one, the tasters were asked to rank the wines as "quality" and "popular." Forty-three percent maintained that the cheap wine was the "quality" wine.

In a referendum that was held in Europe in 2000, people were asked who the most famous wine producer in the world was. The Rothschild family came in first place with a substantial lead. It is worth mentioning that in the American wine market, this family is also a partner of the largest California wine producer.

Wine

The largest wine "cellar" in the world, Ernest and Julio Gallo in Somona, chalks up sales of close to a billion bottles of wine per annum.

Wine

Although it seems self-evident, it is worthwhile repeating the fact that wine in a bottle that is stopped with a cork must be stored "lying down". The wine moistens the cork, thereby preventing oxidation.

Wine

Your lover arrives and you have forgotten to chill the wine you bought? Under no circumstances should you put the bottle of wine in the freezer – the glass is liable to crack. The best solution is an ice-bucket (like the one used for champagne). And incidentally, fast "freezing" or fast "warming" of wine will spoil its taste.

Wine

*U*nfinished bottles of wine can be stored (in the refrigerator) for a few days, but this wine should be used for cooking and not for drinking at the dinner table.

Wine

I have a neighbor who freezes leftover wine (mainly red wine) in sealed plastic bags. She claims that the wine "ice" is excellent for cooking and preparing sauces.

Wine

Red wine is poured into a broad round glass, which is filled to one-third of its capacity.

Wine

Red wine is served at room temperature... as long as it's 18°C/64°F.

Wine

White wine is poured into a tall narrow glass, which is filled to two-thirds of its capacity.

Wine

White wine is served chilled to $12^\circ C / 53^\circ F$.

Wine

 hampagne is served in a tall narrow glass, which is filled to within an inch of the rim.

Wine

Champagne is served chilled to 10°C/50°F. High-quality champagne is chilled to 12°C/53°F, and sometimes to 14°C/57°F. When champagne is chilled to below 8°C/46°F, it "kills" the taste.

Wine

We have already said that an open bottle of champagne can be stored in the refrigerator for a few days. If you do that, you will discover that the champagne loses its bubbles. What can you do? Add a few raisins to the champagne!

Wine

Wine – **The interpretation of wine in a dream** depends on the particular culture: some interpret wine as a sign of abundance, while others see it as a symbol of drunkenness and failure. Usually, dreaming about wine means that the dreamer can expect family celebrations. Drinking wine portends happiness and friendships. Breaking bottles of

wine means that the dreamer's love and passion will almost be excessive. Barrels of wine are a symbol of luxury. Pouring wine from one container to another predicts a variety of pleasures and travels for the dreamer. If the dreamer dreams that he deals in wine, his profession in life will be lucrative. If a young woman dreams of drinking wine, she will marry a rich and respectable man.

Wine

Grapes – **The interpretation of grapes in a dream** symbolize hedonism and the pursuit of pleasure. They are used in feasts and rituals as a symbol of fertility and abundance for what comes from nature (mother earth).

Grapevine – **The interpretation of Grapevine in a dream** is used as an extremely powerful symbol of life and fertility.

Vine – Seeing a vine with grapes **in a dream** indicates hard work that will result in prosperity and great success. Dreaming about vines is a sign of success and joy. Flowering vines signify good health. Dead vines are a warning of failure in an important undertaking. Poisonous vines means that the dreamer will be taken in by a clever scheme, and his health will suffer.

Wine

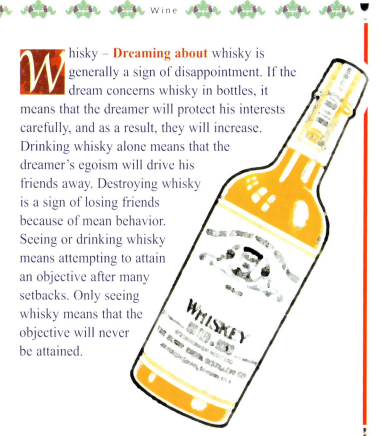

Whisky – **Dreaming about** whisky is generally a sign of disappointment. If the dream concerns whisky in bottles, it means that the dreamer will protect his interests carefully, and as a result, they will increase. Drinking whisky alone means that the dreamer's egoism will drive his friends away. Destroying whisky is a sign of losing friends because of mean behavior. Seeing or drinking whisky means attempting to attain an objective after many setbacks. Only seeing whisky means that the objective will never be attained.

Drinking – **Dreaming about** drinking alcoholic beverages indicates financial loss. If the dreamer sees himself drunk on wine, he can expect great success. Drinking water, however, predicts being let down by someone else.

Wine

Liquor – **Dreaming about** buying liquor means that the dreamer has designs upon property which does not belong to him. Selling liquor is a sign of impending criticism. Drinking liquor means that the dreamer will come into money in a slightly suspicious way, but friends and women will try to get him to spend it on them. Liquor in bottles is a sign of very good fortune. A woman drinking liquor means an easy-going, superficial character and lifestyle, with no jealousy or grudges.

Wine

Alcoholic beverages – If the dreamer is drinking alcoholic beverages, it means that he must beware of being misled.

Wine

Bar (for drinks) – Seeing a bar **in a dream** indicates insecurity and a yearning for a better future. A bar with a bartender signifies that the dreamer longs to throw a party.

Brandy – **Dreaming about** brandy means that although the dreamer will achieve status and wealth, his lack of refinement will preclude friendship with those he most wants to win over.

Wine

*F*rom wine what sudden friendship springs!

John Gay (1685-1732)

143

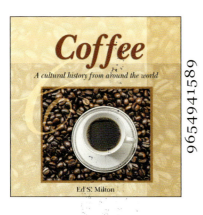
9654941589

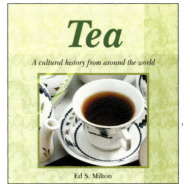
9654941597

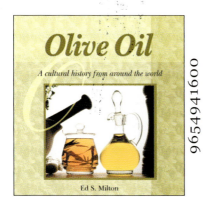
9654941600

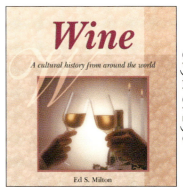
9654941619